W0115867

Old Bones and New Buds

CONTENTS

 **NATIONAL GEOGRAPHIC**

 Hampton-Brown

School Publishing

Words with ew, ui, ou, ue

Look at each picture. Read the words.

Example:

fr**ui**t

resc**ue**

f**ue**l

s**ou**p

j**ew**els

s**ui**t

Key Words

Read the note Ms. Kew wrote to her students. Look at the picture.

February 3

Dear Class,

It's **almost** that time **again** . **Tomorrow** is our field trip! We will leave **between** 8:00 and 8:30. When we get there, you will feel like we **went** way back in time. You will see things that will **surprise** you, things that you will **never** see at **any** other place. **Below** is just one thing we will see. I think your love for really old things will **grow** !

We'll have fun!
Ms. Kew

Where is the class going on their field trip?

GO! **Phonics Games**
NGReach.com

Fossils

by Maria Alvarez

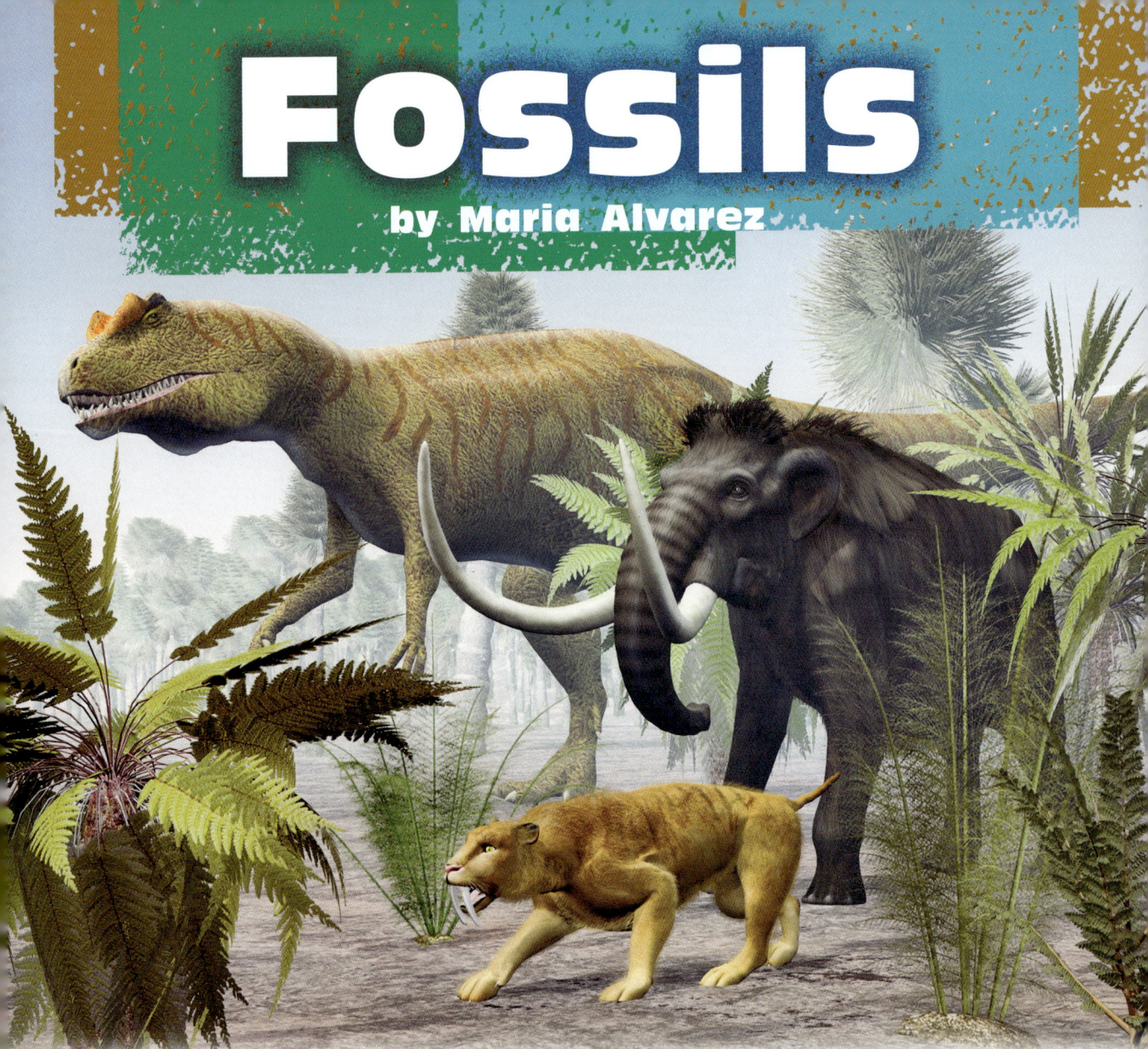

Plants and animals can die out. Many kinds
of changes make this happen.

plant

animal

If plants and animals vanish from Earth, how can you know about them? You find the best clues from fossils.

amber fossil

rock fossil

Fossils are the remains of plants and animals. You see fossils in rocks. You see them in tree sap. The sap was sticky like glue, but then it grew hard. You can also see fossils in amber. They look like jewels.

scientist

Crews of scientists dig for fossils below the earth. They want to find out new things about what used to live on Earth.

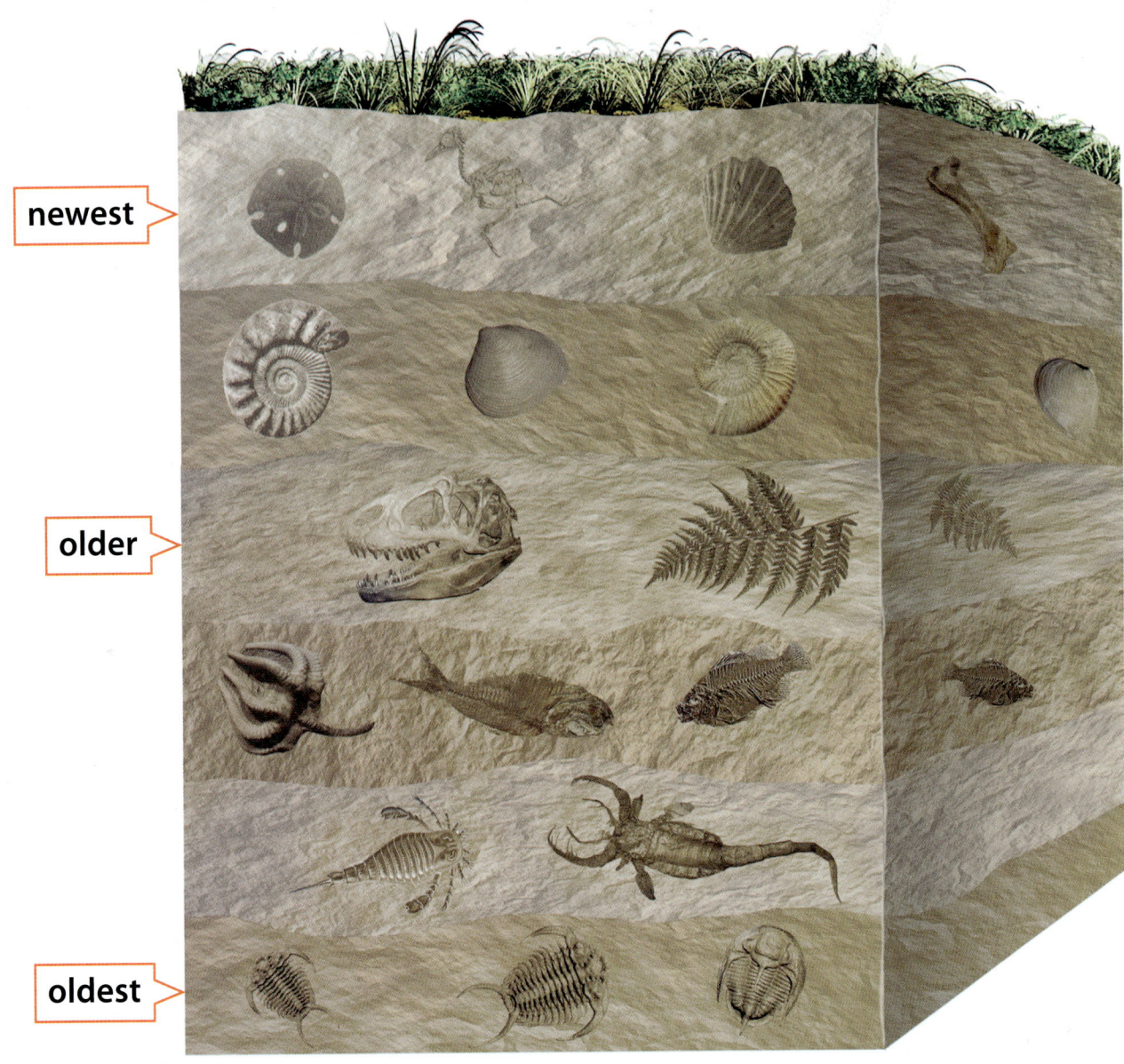

newest

older

oldest

Plants and animals change over time. The age of a rock helps scientists know when a plant or animal lived. They group fossils by age. They can line them up from oldest to newest rocks and see the changes.

You can't bruise fossils, but you can chip them. To rescue fossils, you must never rush. If they're between rocks, you must pry them loose one by one.

The best surprise for a scientist is finding an animal in one piece. A few huge animals were frozen in very cold places.

tar

Other animals had the cruel fate of getting stuck in tar pits. Over time, the tar became as hard as rock. Any trapped animal became a fossil.

Animal tracks are also fossils. Let's say an animal went through a muddy field. Then a big wind blew sand on top of the animal's prints. In time, the muddy earth got as hard as cement. The prints became fossils.

Plants also can make a type of print. Let's say a leaf flew through the air and landed on a soft rock. When the leaf died, it left a black film shaped like itself. The rock got harder. The leaf's print became a fossil.

fruit bat

bamboo

gray wolf

bluebells

Some plants and animals of our time will be the fossils of tomorrow. New plants and animals will grow up, die, and be fossils. Earth keeps changing—again and again and again! ❖

Words with ew, ui, ou, ue

Read these words.

blue	bones	few	fruit	glue	jewel
recruit	soup	spoon	bowl	teeth	youth

Find the words with
ew, ui, ou, or **ue.**
Use letters to build them.

f r u i t

Talk Together

Look at the pictures of things that scientists found at a dig. Choose words from the box above to tell your partner about the items.

They found a *few teeth*.

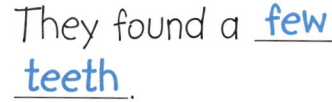

Endings -s, -es, -ed, -ing

Look at each picture. Read the words.

splash**es**

sing**s**

fli**es**

rac**ed**

jump**ed**

hopp**ed**

napp**ing**   rock**ing**

vot**ing**

Key Words

Read each set of sentences. Match the sets to the pictures.

High Frequency Words

again

almost

any

below

between

grow

never

surprise

tomorrow

went

Growing and Mowing

1. These plants are a **surprise**. We did not mean for **any** seeds to fall **between** the cracks.

2. **Tomorrow** we will mow **again**. We **never** got to the field that is **below**.

3. We **went** to see the roses **grow**. **Almost** all the blooms were open!

What would you like to grow?

Phonics Games
NGReach.com

17

Plant Seeds

by Carlos Vazquez

For many animals, life begins with an egg.
For plants, life starts with a seed.

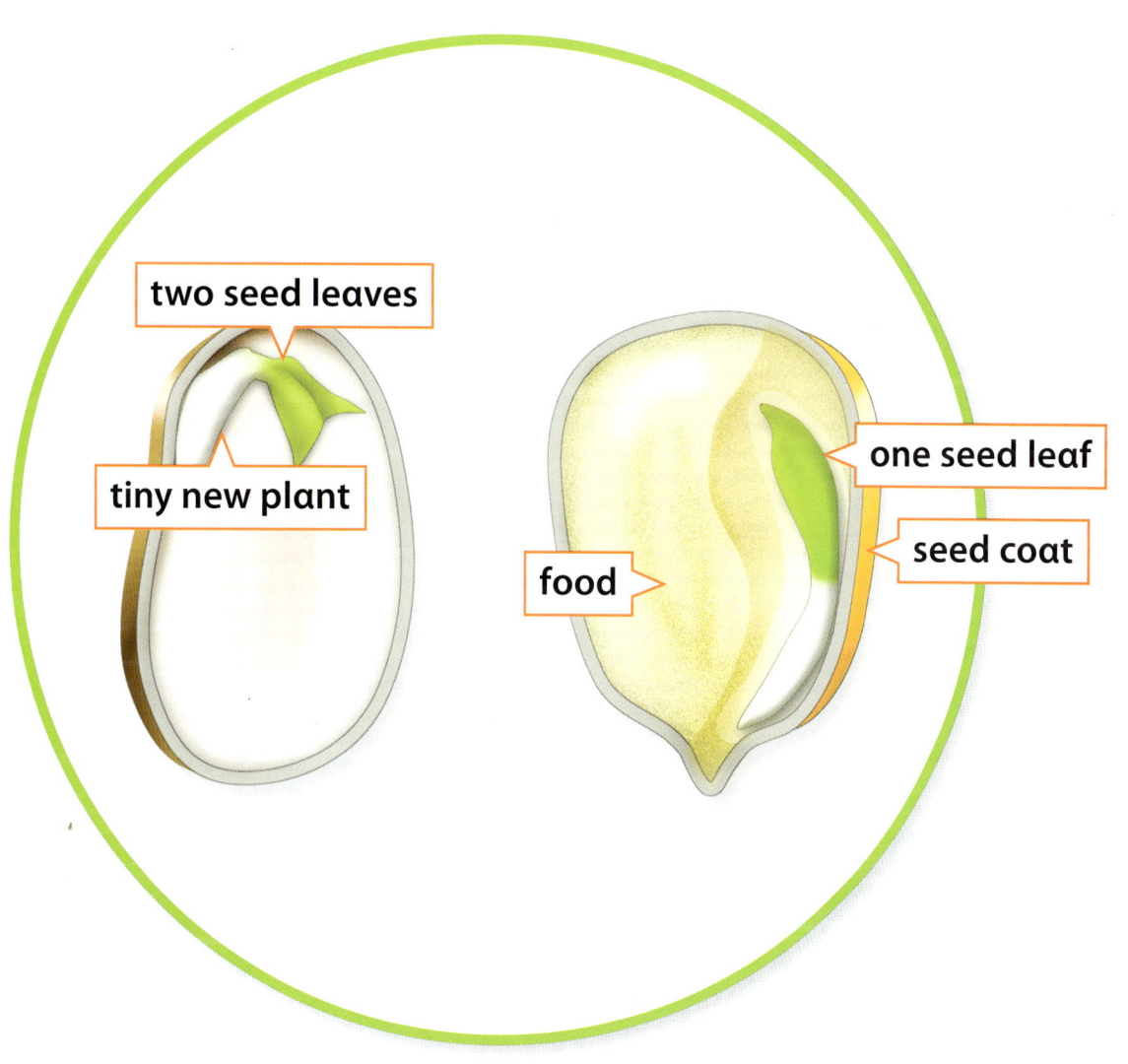

Any seed holds a tiny new plant. It also
contains food. Around the plant and the food
is the seed coat. If you soaked a seed in water,
the seed coat would fall off. Then you could see
one or two seed leaves where the plant and food
are hiding.

Seeds come from the fruits of plants. Fruits can be hard or soft. They can be wrapped in shells or pods.

When a fruit is ripe, the seeds will be released. Lots of fruit can be dropped below a plant. The seeds could never all grow there. Many seeds must be shifted to a new place.

Wind can shift seeds around. Some seeds have wings or silky hairs that make flying on the breeze easy.

Other seeds are very light. It's no surprise that the wind catches them up!

husk

space filled with air

coconut seed

Many plants growing beside water make seeds that can float. These seeds have strong husks. In the seed and the husk is a space filled with air.

Some husks are so strong that the seeds can make it through almost any hard trip. These seeds get tossed about in the sea. If the husks do not crack, the seeds might reach an island!

Animals can shift seeds. As an animal brushes by a plant, seeds cling to its coat. A robin flies by, grabbing a seed between its beak for a snack. The robin may drop the seed before eating. This is how seeds are shifted.

When a seed's trip ends, will the seed grow into a plant tomorrow? Not so fast! Most seeds must be warm and damp below the earth. Then, when the time is right, the tiny plant pushes its way out of the seed coat!

As the plant grows, it makes fruit. Then the seeds begin the trip to new life again. ❖

Endings -s, -es, -ed, -ing

Read these words.

bagging	digs	diving	flies	napping
planted	raked	relaxes	resting	weeding

Find the words with the endings **–s**, **-es**, **-ed**, and **–ing**. Use letters to build them.

d i v i n g

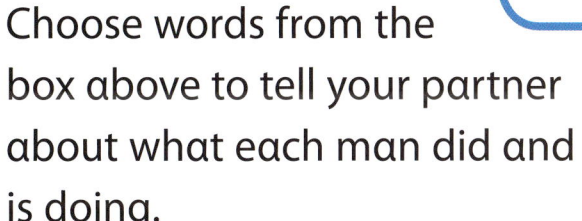

Talk Together

He <u>planted</u>, but now he is <u>weeding</u>.

Choose words from the box above to tell your partner about what each man did and is doing.

True or False?

Work with a partner. Below are statements. Read the first one aloud. Is it true? Read it again, and say true or false. Check the upside-down answer. If you're right, you get a point. The next statement goes to your partner. When you're done, count up points. Who ended up with the most?

An apple is a fruit.

True. An apple is a fruit.

Glue is good for making soup.

False. Glue is not food!

All dinosaurs were cruel and nasty.

False. Some ate plants and were gentle.

You can never make a rock grow bigger.

True. Rocks are not living.

A plane needs fuel to keep flying.

True. Planes need gas just like trucks.

The sun will not rise tomorrow.

False. The sun rises every day.

There are at least 28 days in any month.

True. A month has between 28–31 days.

When people are jogging, they are running as fast as they can.

False. They don't go too fast so they don't get tired.

Acknowledgments

Grateful acknowledgment is given to the authors, artists, photographers, museums, publishers, and agents for permission to reprint copyrighted material. Every effort has been made to secure the appropriate permission. If any omissions have been made or if corrections are required, please contact the Publisher.

Photographic Credits

CVR (b) View Stock RF/age fotostock. (t) WDG Photo/Shutterstock. **2** (bl) Rago Arts/Shutterstock. (br) Artville. (cl) Konstantin Sutyagin/Shutterstock. (ctl) PhotoDisc/Getty Images. (ctr) NikAlex/ Shutterstock. (tl) Tatiana Popova/Shutterstock. (tr) Eyewire. **3** (b) Liz Garza Williams/Hampton-Brown/National Geographic School Publishing. (r) Geoff Hardy/Shutterstock. **6** (b) Jonathan Blair/ National Geographic Image Collection. (t) Paul Mckeown/iStockphoto. **7** O. Louis Mazzatenta/ National Geographic Image Collection. **9** Bianca Lavies/National Geographic Image Collection. **10** Albert Copley/Visuals Unlimited. **12** (inset) University Corporation for Atmospheric Research/ Photo Researchers, Inc. **13** Albert Lleal/Minden Pictures/National Geographic Image Collection. **14** (bl) DLILLC/Corbis. (br) John Woodworth/iStockphoto. (tl) DigitalStock/Corbis. (tr) Simon Oxley/ iStockphoto. **15** (bl) PSD photography/Shutterstock. (cc) Photodisc/Siede Preis/Getty Images. (cl) Thierry Ollivier/Musee Guimet/Getty Images. (cr) John Reader/Photo Researchers, Inc. (l) Digital Image © 2009 Museum Associates / LACMA/Art Resource, Inc. (tr) Liz Garza Williams/Hampton-Brown/ National Geographic School Publishing. **16** (bl) Stockbyte/Getty Images. (br) A. Ramey/PhotoEdit. (cc) John Foxx Images/Imagestate. (cl) pixel shepherd/Alamy Images. (cr) Fancy/Veer/Corbis. (tc) Joel Sartore/National Geographic Image Collection. (tl) Frank Leung/iStockphoto. (tr) Michael Melford/ National Geographic Image Collection. **17** (b) Liz Garza Williams/Hampton-Brown/National Geographic School Publishing. (c) Brand X Pictures/Getty Images. (l) geogphotos/Alamy Images. (r) DigitalStock/ Corbis. (tl) Pefkos/Shutterstock. **18** (b) Global Images/Alamy Images. (tl) FoodCollection/ StockFood America. **20** (bc) FoodCollection/StockFood America. (t, l, br) PhotoDisc/Getty Images. **21** imagebroker/Alamy Images. **22** (t, b) Simon Colmer and Abby Rex/Alamy Images. (l) Dimitri Vervitsiotis/Digital Vision/Getty Images. **23** Joel Sartore/National Geographic Image Collection. **24** Pictor/ ImageState/Alamy Images. **25** (bg) Maria Skaldina/Shutterstock. (inset) PhotoDisc/Getty Images. **26** (bg) PhotoDisc/Getty Images. (inset) Ron Sanford/Photo Researchers, Inc. **27** Creatas/ Jupiterimages. **28** (br) PhotoDisc/Getty Images. (l) Paul Debois/Visuals Unlimited. (tr) yxowert/ Shutterstock. **29** (br) Chris Price/iStockphoto. (cc) Jason Ingram/Alamy Images. (l) Steve Hix/Somos Images/age fotostock. (tr) Liz Garza Williams/Hampton-Brown/National Geographic School Publishing. **31** (tr) Eray Haciosmanoglu/Shutterstock.

Illustrator Credits
4-5, **8**, **11-12**, **19**, **24**, **30-31** Paul Mirocha

The National Geographic Society
John M. Fahey, Jr., President & Chief Executive Officer
Gilbert M. Grosvenor, Chairman of the Board

Copyright © 2011 The Hampton-Brown Company, Inc., a wholly owned subsidiary of the National Geographic Society, publishing under the imprints National Geographic School Publishing and Hampton-Brown.

National Geographic School Publishing
Hampton-Brown
www.NGSP.com

Printed in the USA.
Quad Graphics, Leominster, MA

ISBN: 978-0-7362-8075-4

17 18 19
10 9 8 7